T0067155

Be the Duck...

Tips for Letting Things Roll Off Your Back

KATHY HOFF

BALBOA.
PRESS

A DIVISION OF HAY HOUSE

Balboa Press books may be ordered through booksellers or by contacting:

Balboa Press
A Division of Hay House
1663 Liberty Drive
Bloomington, IN 47403
www.balboapress.com
1 (877) 407-4847

Because of the dynamic nature of the Internet, any web addresses or
links contained in this book may have changed since publication and
may no longer be valid. The views expressed in this work are solely those
of the author and do not necessarily reflect the views of the publisher,
and the publisher hereby disclaims any responsibility for them.

The author of this book does not dispense medical advice or prescribe the use
of any technique as a form of treatment for physical, emotional, or medical
problems without the advice of a physician, either directly or indirectly. The
intent of the author is only to offer information of a general nature to help
you in your quest for emotional and spiritual well-being. In the event you use
any of the information in this book for yourself, which is your constitutional
right, the author and the publisher assume no responsibility for your actions.

Any people depicted in stock imagery provided by Thinkstock are
models, and such images are being used for illustrative purposes only.
Certain stock imagery © Thinkstock.

Print information available on the last page.

ISBN: 978-1-5043-3012-1 (sc)
ISBN: 978-1-5043-3013-8 (e)

Balboa Press rev. date: 03/25/2015

Dedication

Like any endeavor, it takes more than one person to accomplish a dream. In my case, it's taken a tribe, and I am so grateful for my husband, my children, parents and siblings for their support and love throughout my life. They have always made me feel I could do anything I set my mind to. I am also thankful for my teachers – those who have taught be lessons in life, both positive and negative, so I can continue to become the person I am supposed to be.

My appreciation also goes to those who make this a better world through service and kindness! These people – some I know, some I've never met – have been my mentors and examples of how I want to live my life.

Contents

Foreword by Brian Luke Seaward, Ph.D.,
Boulder, Colorado, Author the best-selling
books, *Stand Like Mountain, Flow like Water
and Stressed is Desserts Spelled Backward*.................ix

Preface xi

Introduction xiii

How Do You Handle Stress? 1

Be Still 5

Golfing with Mom..9

What Kayaking Taught Me...13

The Journey of Journaling..15

My Dryer Sings to Me..19

It's a Matter of Perception...23

Calm Water...27

Hot Stones 31

Do You Like Change? 35

Morning Rituals...39

Getting Your Z-z-z-z's 43

It's All in Your Head!..47

Moonstruck...51

Help! There's Too Much on My Plate! 53
A New Year's Resolution..57
What If?..61
Broken Angel Wings 65
It's Positively Possible! 69

Bibliography 73
About the Author...75

Foreword

One of Don Miguel Ruiz's Four Agreements states, "Don't take things personally." This is great advice. In a rapidly changing, stress-filled world, it becomes quite easy to take things personally. The influx of technology, from smart phone to tablets, hasn't helped. In fact, some would argue that the use of iPads, iPhones and androids has derailed much of our civility to the point that experts in the field of sociology cite narcissism (not to mention basic rudeness) as a serious social problem. What's the solution? For starters, consider letting things roll off your back. Be the Duck. This is sage advice and regardless of how it is expressed (remember the phrase – Don't sweat the small stuff?), we need to hear it over and over again.

Kathy has assembled a wonderful ensemble of stories that do just this. Individually and collectively, these stories are an important reminder to find your center of gravity in a stress-filled world and remain centered through the winds of change. Stories serve both as map and compass to help direct us home (a metaphor for homeostasis or inner peace).

Letting things roll off your back is another way to release, detach, cleanse or surrender and move on with your life. When all else fails to deal with stress, remember, it all comes down to ego.

So consider reading a story a night to end your day on a good note. Let the vibrations of this collective wisdom guide your dreams so that when you awake each day you are refreshed and ready to conquer the world. Use the symbol of the duck as your totem animal to navigate you through the shoals of human trials and challenges... and you will be all the better for it.

Brian Luke Seaward, Ph.D.
Boulder, Colorado
Author the best-selling books, *Stand Like Mountain, Flow like Water* and *Stressed is Desserts Spelled Backward.*

Preface

Once a teacher, always a teacher! Every job I held after teaching elementary school involved training others, and I love sharing information that helps people. Having worked in education and then healthcare, I saw what stress employees were under. It was taking a toll on people's health. Thus started my journey on building my skill set so I could be of service.

After getting my certification to be a Stress Management Trainer from Paramount Institute, I started offering classes at hospitals, and soon was asked to do them elsewhere. A year after that, I was fortunate enough to be able to get a certification from Wellcoaches as a Health and Wellness Coach. Coaching is where I saw firsthand that everyone goes through something!

Be the Duck…Tips for Letting Things Roll off Your Back is the next step in my journey to assist others on their road to wellness, supporting them in learning skills to move from a stress response to a relaxation response. These strategies can start anyone on the road to better health – mind, body, and spirit – if they are willing to take the first step.

My wish for you is to the best version of yourself you can be. Use the motto, "Be the Duck," and see where it takes you!

Introduction

Congratulations on picking up *Be the Duck…Tips for Letting Things Roll off Your Back!* I truly believe there is a reason you were drawn to this title, whether just curiosity or the need to learn more about managing your stress.

Just as you reached out to see what it was all about, I'm reaching out to you with a series of true, short stories that I hope will resonate with you, each holding a tip that you can put into practice. I'm no different from you, as I struggle with my stressors every day. *Be the Duck…Tips for Letting Things Roll off Your Back* is about what I've learned so far. Sit back, relax, and let these words be absorbed into your being as wellness strategies.

How Do You Handle Stress?

How do you handle stress? Does this sound familiar? Feeling sad? Eat chocolate! Problems at work? Brownies will do the trick! Worried about finances? A batch of cookies will make you feel better!

Actually, all stress is not bad. For example, planning a wedding can be stressful but it's a joyful occasion, as is having a new baby or buying a house. This type of stress is called eustress.

There are things that happen around us or on the other side of the world that we don't worry about. We are neutral to them. This is neustress.

Some stress can be motivating like studying for a test that is important to your grade or career or working extra hours to see a project completed. It's when stress becomes constant that it affects your mind, body and spirit. This is Distress! Uninterrupted stress causes your heart rate to go up and immune system to go down. It's the cause of many gastrointestinal problems, headaches and backaches. The stress hormone cortisol is released into your blood stream causing your muscles to become tight. Your circulation slows down, and…shall I go on? I bet you are ready for some pie!

One thing to keep in mind is what stresses you may not stress your spouse or co-workers. Stress is very individual, as are the strategies to help you become more resilient to stress.

The good news is if you break this 'stress response' and move into a 'relaxation response' even for a few minutes a day, you can restore your health. So what is a 'relaxation response'? It's something you do that relaxes your mind and body. Here are some strategies you might try:

- Deep Breathing: This is probably the best tip I can give you! Slow down three or four times a day and take slow, deep breathes – in through the nose and out through your mouth. Try to focus only on your breath.
- Get Moving: Yes, exercise is a fabulous stress buster! It can be bicycling, pickle ball, swimming, dancing, yoga, walking or anything that gets your heart rate up.
- It's sad to say, but desserts aren't really good for stress. Eating nutrient-dense, whole foods will give your body the fuel it needs to fight off stress, keeping your blood sugar levels even, muscles supple, and your memory at its best.

- Do what you enjoy! It can be a hobby, reading, a hot bath, a massage, socializing with friends and family, nature, music, or anything that takes your mind away from your worries for a bit.

Now, if you'll excuse me, my kale chips are waiting for me!

Be the Duck Tip…Have a plan. When you feel stress coming on, select a strategy that works for you and put it into action.

Be Still

If you knew me when I was a child, you would get a kick out of me telling you today that my mantra is "Be Still." Being the oldest of six active children, we were constantly putting on shows for the neighbors, waterskiing at the Lake of the Ozarks, playing sandlot baseball, or roller skating in our garage. I've always had a lot of energy, and along with that comes what I call a 'monkey mind'. My mind continuously was swinging from one idea to another, deciding how to organize projects or put on a fundraising event, but mainly I did a lot of worrying about things I couldn't control. It was sometimes hard to shut it off and fall asleep at night.

When I learned about meditation, I gave it a try. Man, was it hard for me to sit still and try to just breathe. I started with only five minutes a day. I'd fidget, my mind would wonder, and I couldn't wait for the time to be over. But I kept at it. After a few weeks, I noticed a calmness starting to replace my constant thoughts. Then I slowly added a few minutes each week to my meditation time and started using the mantra "Be Still' as a cue to myself when I felt worry or agitation starting up.

The benefits for me of practicing meditation were that I was calmer and things that used to bother me started to just roll of my back – like a duck. A duck's feathers are oiled so water will not go through them or saturate them by rain. There is an oil-making gland on the duck's back near the tail. The duck spreads a film of this oil all over the surface of its feathers. Now oil and water will not mix, so the water cannot get through this oil to wet the duck's feathers. That's how I look at meditation. It's time invested as a protection so stressors can't get through to me. The effects are not immediate, but by practicing meditation daily, we can become a well-oiled duck!

There are many forms of meditation, and it's been around for thousands of year. Meditation is even taught in some schools because it has been proven to reduce stress, strengthen the immune system, improve relationships at school and home, decrease aggressiveness and anxieties, improve behavior, attitude, focus, memory and concentration. You can meditate by just focusing on your breath, concentrating on words like my mantra 'Be Still', pray, give attention to releasing tension in your body, do guided mediation, visualization, paint, listen to calming music, or practice walking meditation, just to name a few.

*Be the Duck Tip...*I highly recommend meditation as a practice to help manage your stressors – whatever they may be. It's also a very beneficial skill to pass on to children in your life. If we do this, maybe the next generation won't have as many 'monkey minds'.

Golfing with Mom

Playing on the Lakewood Golf Course has always been a dream of my mom's. She played plenty of other golf courses and participated on several women's leagues, but no one had ever invited her to play at Lakewood. She was so excited when my husband and I moved to Lakewood, thinking she would finally get a chance to play on our beautiful course. So, for Mother's Day, I gave her a hand-made gift certificate to play golf with me here.

I thought mom would be elated, but she expressed worry that I hadn't played golf in seven years and she was pretty sure I would need to practice before embarrassing both of us. I mentioned that if I had any good swings in me, I didn't' want to waste them on practice. So, we played!

Did I mention my mother is a spunky 82? She also has a great set of golf clubs, at least ten times better than my old, heavy set. And, wow, can she hit with those clubs! On the 4th hole, she asked me if I had ever used her clubs. I said I hadn't. Then she let me try out her driver. Guess what? I outdrove her. That didn't set too favorably! No more sharing of her clubs! Bless her heart, Mom would forget she had offered me her driver and would ask me again the same question three different times. So three times in 18 holes, I outdrove my mom! We had such a great time just being together, having fun, and setting a date for the next time!

This experience reminded me that if we concentrate our time and energy on what we value (and "family" is one of my values), it can be relaxing, taking our mind off our busy world. So what are your values? What makes you feel alive and rejuvenated? What activity makes you forget about time and live totally absorbed in the moment? It could be gardening, golfing, teaching children, music, creating beauty, building with your hands, physical activity, yoga, spirituality, family, volunteering, a thirst for knowledge, a sense of commitment, perseverance – the list is endless. I encourage you to make a list of your values.

Next, ask yourself, "Am I spending my energies on my values?" Think about your last week.

- How many times did you do something you valued?
- How did you feel about that?
- What barriers do you have that keep you from doing what you really want to do?
- How can you get around them?
- What went well last week?
- How can you use your strengths to get in more valuable times?

This will take some thinking on your part, but it will truly be worth it.

Be the Duck Tip...Make each day count in your life. Do the things you really enjoy with the people who are important to you. I know I will...maybe I will see you on the golf course!

What Kayaking Taught Me

Learning to kayak the year I turned 39 (again) was a goal of mine that gave me more than I was expecting. Getting into the kayak off of a dock without falling in was the first accomplishment, and I was feeling pretty good about my maiden voyage. Since it was my first time out, I stayed close to shore – just in case. But, the water was calm, and

I was gliding along on a small lake feeling relaxed. What a great way to unwind, I thought.

Then I heard it - a speed boat making a large loop around the lake! That means waves! I wasn't ready for those yet, but ready or not, they were headed toward my small orange kayak. I had actually selected the color so it could be seen while I was in it and if it flipped over. Good planning, Kathy.

Do I hit the waves head on or sideways? Hadn't thought that one through! Okay, sideways, just float over the top of them. My boat rocked up and down and I rode the waves, actually very calming. I had this! But on a small lake, the waves hit the shore and then bounce back out. Now they were coming from both sides. All I could do was ride it out.

My first merit badge! I made it through and kept going, all the way around the 80 acre lake. It gave me time to think about life, and I realized life is much like the unexpected waves. Obstacles come at us and we worry about how to handle them. We stress that there might be more coming. But learning to recognize them, go with the flow, and get through them is quite an accomplishment.

Be the Duck Tip… Problems don't last forever; it's how we handle them that makes the difference.

The Journey of Journaling

It was very common when I was growing up for girls to have diaries where they would write about the cute boy in home room, the frustration of having your sister wear your new jeans without asking, and, of course, the dream of who was going to ask you to prom. The diary always had a key so its secrets could be locked away (or picked open with a bobby pin in some cases).

The actual act of writing is healing in that your emotions can pour out freely, without judgment. Then in rereading your thoughts, you can learn more about yourself. What makes you sad or what gives you joy? You grow personally simply by writing.

Today many call this journaling – writing down your thoughts and ideas. Get them from your head and heart to paper (or chalkboard, computer, or café napkins). Anyone can journal, and the only rule is that there are no rules. You can say what you want, not worry about correct spelling or punctuation, draw pictures if you prefer, and do as often as you like.

The benefits of journaling are many.

- As mentioned before, personal growth can come from reflecting on your previous entries. You'll gain insights about your moods and how you act.
- Journaling can be a stress-reliever. Through writing, you can let go of what bothers you. Get it off your chest. Some people even take it so far as to take what they wrote, wad it up and toss it in the trash can or fireplace as a symbolic release of the stressor.
- For some people, art can go deeper than words. Art journaling is using drawings, painting, photography or any other media you want, allowing you to express yourself.
- Looking back through journal entries can give you a look at your past. This can lead to more compassion for yourself and more empathy for others as you try to understand your motives, perceptions, and goals.
- Journaling can help you process failed relationships, guilt, grief, and loss.
- Natural journals are collections of bits of nature or recording what you notice about nature. Focus on what gives you wonder. Use that knowledge to surround yourself with things you love – leaves, fresh flowers, or smooth stones.
- Gratitude journals include entries about people and things you are thankful for. You can appreciate the good things as well as the frustrating things,

because you can learn and grow from both. This type of journal is great for retrospect and understanding that there is balance in your life, and a lot of it is wonderful.

*Be the Duck Tip...*As I said, there are no rules, but many benefits. These are just a few suggestions for you to reap the benefits of journaling. Writing is simple, and you can start with just a few minutes a day. Go ahead, start on your journey of journaling.

My Dryer Sings to Me

My new dryer actually hums me a tune every time the clothes are dry, continues the constant reminders, and finally, when I open the door, it rejoices with a final tune! And so do I - it will quit playing that annoying song!

I've tried to figure out why this bothers me so much. Maybe it's because I didn't choose the tune or perhaps because it repeats itself over and over. Possibly I find it disturbing because it is telling me what to do - empty the dryer. The bottom line is I don't have any control over it, as I don't know how to turn it off (because my husband washed the directions with a load of clothes). Yes, I am blaming someone else!

Most people like to have control over their lives. They even have expectations of what "other" people should say, what to eat, how to act, who to love, and what friends and family members are supposed to do for a living. They find it frustrating and stressful when other folks don't behave how they think they should.

When people realize they don't really have control of what others do or say, they can find a little more contentment and feel less stressed. Truth be known, individuals only can be responsible for how they act themselves. This awareness and change in thoughts is actually good for our health. When people feel stressed, real or perceived, the body releases cortisol, a stress hormone, which affects the body in negative ways. Other "stress" signals noticed in the body are tight muscles in the neck and shoulders, shallow breathing, headaches, gastrointestinal problems, and lower back pain, just to name a few. So you see, it only does damage to the person trying to control others.

If trying to control what others do has been a habit of yours and you want to change this for your health's sake, realize it will take some time to create new habits.

- First, make a list with two columns, one being what you can control and the second what you can't. Fill in the columns.
- Next, in order to create a different habit rather than trying to control others, try the A-B-C Method.
    - A – **Acknowledge** the thought as it comes in your head
    - B – Take a deep **Breath**
    - C – **Choose** a more positive thought about that person to replace the controlling thought you started with. When you fill that void, you will be on your way to changing the way you think.

And remember, it takes about 21 repetitions to create a new habit, so if you slip up, just keep trying and be forgiving of yourself.

Now, if anyone has the directions on how to turn off the constant singing of my dryer, please send them my way. I'm stressing out!

Be the Duck Tip...So, if you want to change trying to control others, you must change your thinking habits. Changing your thoughts can change your life! Realize that...

Our THOUGHTS create our FEELINGS,
Our FEELINGS create our ACTIONS,
And our ACTIONS create our RESULTS.

It's a Matter of Perception

You've probably heard it said that a person's perception is their reality. It's what they believe to be true. This reminds me of when I was teaching 6th graders. I loved this age group because the children were curious, trying to figure out how they fit into this world, and squirrely as heck!

Anyway, one writing assignment I gave was to write a short story about a personal experience that included at least one other person. The second part of the assignment was for them to ask one of the people in their story to write about the same experience, without sharing their own version, and bring both to class.

Talk about some great stories! Besides looking for correct grammar and punctuation, I was hoping to show how people can view the same experience differently, depending on their scope of reference, the environment they were raised, and their values.

The one story that stands out is when Justin wrote about fishing with his dad and how awesome it was to spend all morning with him. He even caught the biggest fish ever – as long as his arm. It was the best day of his life!

Dad wrote about the same fishing trip and how it was such a sleepy experience with mosquitos constantly swarming and biting them. They only caught one small fish, so small they had to throw it back.

See what I mean? People see things differently. This really touched my heart about "truths." Your truth is your perception. Your perception is your truth. If you think about this and realize it when you are talking to co-workers, your family, friends, people you just met, or people on the news, it helps you understand that they may not be wrong; they just see things differently. Their perception is there truth. Let that soak in for a minute. It really helps in not judging others.

Not only does everyone have a different perception of events in life, but everyone has a story – the positive and the negatives that they deal with. We aren't always privy to someone else's story. This is where compassion and empathy come into play. We should consider offering these to others and feel blessed when someone offers these virtues to us without knowing what we are dealing with.

As a health and wellness coach, I can attest to this truth. Everyone, and I mean every single person I have the privilege of coaching, is dealing with something big. I really admire how people work through these things and become resilient, bouncing forward into their life again.

Be the Duck Tip...No one is promised a perfect life. We all have our own reality, our own perception of that reality, and our own ways of getting through them. I think if we just recognize and honor that fact about ourselves and others, we'll be doing a great service to mankind.

Calm Water

Have you really looked at a body of water, a lake, or a pond that is really calm? Not just seeing the surface, but what's floating on top of the water like a fall leaf or a bug with its legs sprawled out appearing to walk on water? And what about the reflections you see on the water? Clouds, tall grasses, or mountains? Then look a little deeper. What do you see below the surface? If it's clear, you might see a fish, an old log or mossy growth. If it's murky, maybe you just see more murkiness.

Did you know that a body of water like a lake or pond turns over twice a year? It's a naturally occurring process of temperature inversion due to changing of atmospheric temperatures. The change in surface water temperatures cause a cycling of water that brings colder or warmer water (depending on the season) up from the bottom, usually disturbing what may have settled during the previous months. After this takes place, the temperatures even out again until there is another major atmospheric change. So there is constant change due to external circumstances.

I'd venture to say that people are very much like bodies of water. Sure, I understand we are mainly made up of water, but when a person looks calm on the surface, we don't always know what they are suppressing deep inside themselves. Are they full of stress, worry, or joy? Or are they full at all? We can't always tell.

We often judge a person by first impression – what we see on the surface. We may see a person's clothes, their body language, their smile or scowl. What can we learn about that person by their outward appearance? Is it real or a mask? Do we really know?

Many times people are a reflection of their environment. People learn their responses to stress by age eight. Their family, culture, school and neighborhood all contribute to that. Unless consciously changed, it's fair to say that many people mirror what they learned as a child.

Look deeper and try to learn about another person. Everyone is dealing with something! You may not always be aware of what it is, but getting to know a person better and listening to them helps you understand them. On the other hand, you may never know what someone is really like. Maybe they are filled with vision and loveliness at the moment or maybe they are battling dragons. Be kind – we never know what lies below the surface.

And like water in a pond turning over, people can change. They age. They become wiser. What used to lay below the surface, can come out in their personality. They can take on a different persona because of personal or professional growth. When someone makes a shift in their outlook on life from negative to positive, you will see that shift. When someone turns over a new leaf, like from a bad habit or addiction, you will notice that change. The waters shift – turns over. When the water temperatures settles back down, you can notice the lasting changes.

Be the Duck Tip...Next time you are quick to form a first impression of someone, whether positive or negative, take a moment and think about this simple water analysis. Is what you see really who they are? Do you understand where they came from? What they've experienced? Do you know what they are dealing with in their private lives? When you look at folks in this way, it opens your mind and heart. My hope is people do the same for you. Wouldn't that be wonderful?

Hot Stones

What would happen if you picked up a stone right out of a fire to throw at someone? Right! You would burn your hand. What would happen if you held on to the hot stone for a long time? You'd probably end up with third degree burns, lose some skin, and have to go the emergency room.

Anger isn't wrong, but holding on to anger is like holding on to a hot stone. It doesn't hurt the person you intended to throw the stone at, only the person holding it. To be emotionally well, you must be able to recognize and express your emotions and control them, and not let them control you. It's the difference between picking up a hot stone and immediately dropping it or holding on to it for the amount of time it takes to aim at someone else or stew about it for days, maybe years. You'll get burned!

Statistics show that uncontrolled anger can contribute to coronary heart disease and ulcers. You've probably seen people get so angry that they get red in the face, clinch their fists, and yell at other people because those folks didn't meet the expectation the angry person had of them. An example of this is road rage. When a driver pulls out too slowly or doesn't take off fast enough when the light changes, there are drivers that will honk, yell, and chase down the other driver. Definitely, misdirected anger. Or have you witnessed a long line at the grocery store because the check-out person is new and has to request management assistance, and someone waiting gets angry at the clerk? Uncontrolled anger.

In these instances, the angry person just doesn't let it go. In fact, they probably talk about it later in the day, getting angrier every time they tell the story, which only reinforces their anger. The cycle continues as the person begins having stress symptoms including increased heart rate and shallow breathing. They may experience irrational thoughts such as other people 'make' them late, other people are inept and shouldn't be in the jobs they have or be allowed to have a driver's license, or other people are just plain stupid. This all leads to more stress and anger.

Here are some steps you can take to monitor and correct these type of behaviors in yourself.

- Understand what makes you feel angry.
- How does your anger express itself? Is it through guilt, rage, impatience, envy, or silence? Do you throw things, punch walls, yell, or cry?
- Know that feeling anger is natural, but how you express it is in your control.

- Think about what unmet expectation you had.
- Was it rational thinking?
- Did you understand the entire situation, or were there things you didn't know about before making your judgment?
- Plan ahead. Re-script your thoughts. For example, if you say, "They always treat me that way, and I don't like it," you can change the words in your head to be, "They usually treat me okay, but this time it wasn't good customer service. It will probably be better next time."
- Use cues to yourself to change your thoughts. You can snap your fingers every time you notice yourself having irrational anger thoughts. Then redirect your thoughts to the positive.
- You can do some deep breathing to break the thoughts.
- Do some jumping jacks, take a walk, work out or do something to allow the stress of anger to drain from your body.
- Have a support person or two you can go to when you need help redirecting your anger. Be sure these folks don't fuel the fire where the stones are, but are good at showing you how to drop the stones.
- Develop realistic expectations of yourself and others.
- Practice kindness and forgiveness of yourself and others.

Be the Duck Tip...Practicing strategies that work for you will give you peace of mind and less stress on your body. Controlling our emotions like anger is healthy for your wellbeing, just like practicing yoga, running, eating healthy, and meditating. In fact, the only hot stones I want are those used on my back during a massage!

Do You Like Change?

It has been said by someone much wiser than me that, "The only person who likes change is a baby with a wet diaper!" However, I've always gravitated toward change – no I'm not back in diapers...yet! I've enjoyed changing jobs in my career so I could encounter new challenges and learn new skills. By moving to different neighborhoods or joining different organizations, I've had the opportunity to meet new people. Mixing up activities that I do for pleasure keeps me from getting bored and exercise different muscles. Notice all of these changes are ones that I 'selected'. I bet you are similar in thinking – change is good as long as you initiate it!

But notice your responses when change is introduced by someone else. For example, a supervisor wants to change a process without inviting your input first; the menu at your favorite restaurant has changed and your go-to meal is no longer on it; gas prices go up again; or .....(You fill in the blank). People don't like change so much under these circumstances.

Change isn't easy, especially when it comes to things like moving from your home to a nursing home, getting over a major loss, or having your sales territory cut in half while working on a commission basis. So how do you handle change? Do you gripe, withdraw, and fight it tooth-and-nail? Does it stress you?

Here are some suggestions you might try to help make "change" a little less stressful:

- Recognize what you can and cannot control. No sense beating your head against a brick wall if all you're going to get from it is a headache!
- Look for the positive in the change. Everything that happens has a silver lining or at least a shred of good merit. Seek that out.
- Change your thoughts. Once you've found the 'good' in the change, start focusing on that instead of thinking 'poor me' or 'it's not fair'. Life isn't always fair, so find a way to make lemonade out of lemons, as my mom would say.
- Hang out around like-minded, positive people. Find others who look for the best in change instead of gossiping about how bad it is. This will move you forward in life rather than weighing you down like a pair of concrete shoes.
- Finally, embrace the change. You've found some benefits to it, you've focused on the positive and been uplifted by others who think similarly, now put action to your thoughts. Do things that

will make the change easier. Maybe that means introducing yourself to others or inviting them to eat with you at the nursing home, writing thank you notes to folks that have helped you through a rough time, or seek to find new clients who really need your products and services.

*Be the Duck Tip...*So instead of crying like a wet baby, adjust and embrace change. Growth only happens through change. Some of it is painful, some is enjoyable, but all of it is a part of life.

Morning Rituals

Here's a simple way to start your day, even if you only have a couple of minutes. It is actually a habit I developed because I found I was having trouble focusing on my goals of managing stress in my life and helping others learn to cope with stress in theirs. Every morning, even before my feet hit the floor, I answer these four questions.

- What am I thankful for?
- What is one thing I am going to do today that nourishes myself?

- What is one thing I am going to do today that will nourish someone else?
- What will be my mantra for the day?

Maybe you have other questions you'd like to pose to yourself that would help you reach your goals. You might write them down, memorize them and/or create a form or spot in your journal where you can record your responses.

Perhaps you prefer to write in a gratitude journal as a morning ritual. Many people have found this to be a helpful tool in appreciating what they have and where they are in life. It's a way to focus on the positive side of things in your life.

If you like music, you might set your alarm or phone to a soothing music selection that wakes you up gently so you can greet the day in a calm manner.

Some people like to read from inspirational books, offering words of wisdom to live by for the day.

Another option is to mentally scan your body and see how it feels. Are there any areas of stress? If so, do some deep breathing exercises before getting out of bed. Stretching is also another great way to wake up your body.

If you try any of these, the next step is to make it a habit. Research shows it takes about 21 recurrences to create a new habit. So keep practicing until it becomes second nature to you. If you forget a day or two, oh, well, just start back up. It's okay. Don't beat yourself up over it; just begin again the next day.

Be the Duck Tip...Create a morning ritual and notice the difference in how you feel, how you handle difficulties that come your way, how your day goes and how your goals get accomplished.

Getting Your Z-z-z-z's

Do you have trouble falling asleep or staying asleep? Are you kept awake by a snoring partner or pet? Do you wake up feeling like you never rested? This was happening to me as my dog, who sleeps right next to by shoulder, was getting up one to two times a night to go outside to do his business. Then I'd give him a treat and put him back in bed. Guess what? He started getting up more often, sometimes four times a night! Something had to give. I finally learned from a fellow dog-lover that my dog understood the treats to be a reward for going outside so he was doing it to please me and get an extra treat. Well, we got that solved rather quickly, and I was back to getting more z-z-z-z's.

Back to the topic! Lack of a good night's sleep is a real health problem, as it increases the risks of heart disease, obesity, diabetes, depression, and high blood pressure, just to name a few. It also contributes to auto and work accidents, lack of focus, lower productivity in the workplace, added stress, and basically a lower quality of life. Did you know that there are more car accidents caused by drowsy drivers than drunk drivers? Scary, isn't it?

So, sleep is not just a luxury, it's a necessity! A lot of important functions go on in our brain and body while we sleep.

- Our long-term memories and new information are filed away for future reference.
- Our cells renew and repair.
- Our immune system is replenished.
- Hormones are distributed to the proper parts of our body.
- And much more…

The National Sleep Foundation recommends seven to nine hours a night for most adults. So if you feel you are not getting enough z-z-z-z's, here are some suggestions that may help.

- Keep your bedroom technology-free. The latest research shows that electromagnet rays are emitted into your room, even when the technology is turned off, interfering with your natural biorhythms and circadian rhythms. The technology includes computers, televisions, iPads, and all of those other wonderful gadgets we think we can't live without. Truth is, we can't sleep with them.

- Create a bedtime routine so your brain understands when it's time to sleep. Maybe it's turning down the lights, turning off the television, taking a hot bath, reading a good book (not on your Kindle or iPad), doing some yoga stretches or whatever you find relaxing.

- Turn lights out when you go to bed. Even a small amount of light can send the message to your brain that it's daylight, not night time.

- Set your thermostat so your room is cool, yet comfortable.

- Also, use cozy bedding and clothing. Whether it's cotton or flannel, whatever fabric you find most comfortable, use that for your sheets and pajamas.

- Listen to calming music, white noise like a fan, or keep it quiet in your room – whatever relaxes you.

- Don't sleep with children or pets (oops for me!). They may cause you to wake up more often.

- Try to go to bed at the same time and wake up at the same time every day, even on weekends.

- Avoid strenuous exercise at least two hours before bedtime.
- Eating a big meal and/or drinking alcohol late in the evening may cause you to not sleep well. Even if a drink puts you to sleep, you may find that you wake up in the middle of the night.
- Drink chamomile tea.
- Lavender is a calming scent you can use in your bath, on your pillow, or in your lotion.

Sleep is more difficult for those who do shift-work or work nights, people who travel for their job, and moms and dads who have babies. And some folks have more severe sleep problems like narcolepsy or sleep apnea. If you have more than an occasional sleepless night and you've tried some of these strategies, you may want to contact your physician.

Be the Duck Tip...Getting a good night's sleep is so important to your health, both short-term and long-term. It merits your efforts, as the benefits are a much better quality of life. So, what strategy will you try so you can feel rested, sharp, and getting the z-z-z-z's your body and mind require?

It's All in Your Head!

There is more fact than fiction in the statement, "It's all in your head." Yes, your thoughts are responsible for how your body responds to stress. Let me give you some examples.

When you feel stressed (and remember that stress is very individual - what stresses me may not stress you), your body reacts. It pumps adrenaline and cortisol into the bloodstream so you can focus on an immediate response to your stress. This is one reaction and part of what is called the 'fight or flight' response. Cortisol is a hormone that can turn off inflammation, however, chronic stress actually desensitizes the cells and causes inflammation to go crazy! This can create chronic inflammation leading to joint pain, damaging your blood vessels and brain cells, leading to insulin resistance and more.

If that isn't enough bad news, here is more. When stressed, your heart rate goes up, your immune system goes down, you may experience back and neck pain, headaches, gastrointestinal problems, memory issues, weight gain, sleep deprivation, and depression, just to name a few of the serious effects of chronic stress. These are called 'stress responses."

If that doesn't get your attention, listen to this. Your body doesn't know if your stress is real or perceived. If you think it, your body will respond as if it is happening. Here's a personal story that reflects this fact.

When my daughter was 16, her curfew on the weekends was midnight. One night, she was late. It was 12:10 and I hadn't heard from her. (Keep in mind this was before everyone had a cell phone!) I was getting angry. Then 12:15, 12:20 rolled around, and I started to get worried. In fact, my breathing became shallow and I was starting to sweat. By 12:30, I just knew she'd been in a car accident and was in a ditch somewhere. I got sick to my stomach, my heart hurt, and I could hardly breathe. Then she walked in the door. "Sorry, Mom, I forgot to call."

Then when she was 19, it really did happen. She was in a terrible car accident. I was out of state at the time and received the call from my son. It was going to take ten hours to get there. I was told my daughter had several injuries and was in a head trauma unit at a hospital. Talk about stress! Guess what? My body responded exactly as it did when I 'thought' she had been in an accident. It's our body's way of coping with stress. Most of our blood flow goes towards our core getting us ready to respond to the trauma we are thinking about. The happy ending to this story is that she made it through and today is the momma of triplets!

The good news is even if you are stressed to the max, you have the opportunity to shift from the stress response to the relaxation response by changing your thoughts. That's right! Just by interrupting your stressful and negative thoughts, you can restore your health and learn to 'Be the Duck.'

Once you identify what your stressors are, start noticing where your body feels the stress. Maybe it's a tight neck, shallow breathing, or a tightness in your chest. At that point, acknowledge it, and change your thoughts to positive ones.

This can be done using several methods. They are not hard, but they will take some practice to change your patterns of thinking. Remember, it takes about 21 repetitions to change a habit, and that holds true for your thoughts, too.

- Reframe your thoughts. For example, if you always tell yourself, "I never do anything right," shift your thinking to something like, "I do lots of things right and I'll use this as a learning opportunity."
- Wear a rubber band on your wrist. Every time you notice a negative thought, snap the rubber band (take it easy – no pain) or switch it to the other

wrist. This brings your attention to the moment and your thoughts.

- Come up with a few positive affirmations that mean something to you and write them on post-it notes. Place those notes where you will see them several times a day.

Be the Duck Tip…There are a lot of other strategies you can incorporate into your life to shift from the stress response to the relaxation response like exercise, meditation, and breathing exercises. However, it all starts with your thoughts. So the next time you hear someone say, "It's all in your head," you'll know there is truth in that statement!

Moonstruck

Old wives' tales are passed along as food for thought from one generation to the next. My Grandma Martha never gave her opinion whether they were true or not, but she would weave the web of mystery by telling the tales with a gleam in her eye and a smile on her face. Not a full grin, but her lips turning up slightly where top meets bottom, with a hint of possibility.

There were many stories. One such tale was if a person wanted to get rid of moles or freckles on their body, they would tie a knot in a piece of string for each mole or freckle they wished to disappear. Then the string had to be hidden under a rock outside. When the string rotted, the moles would disappear!

Another was cutting hair according to the moon phases. During certain times, if hair was cut at a certain phase of the moon, it would grow back faster. If cut during other phases, it wouldn't grow as fast, thus saving on the cost of a haircut. I understand now as an adult that this goes along with the Farmers' Almanac and is true.

My favorite, though, was the idea of being moonstruck. Grandma had told stories of how people would sleep in the light of a full moon from the time it came up until it was absent from the sky. It had to strike the person's face during this entire time in order for the magic to work. If all these variables were met, then the person might get up and do all their housework, sew a dress, knit a scarf, plow a field or chop wood for the fireplace. The tales were always incredible, especially the part where the person didn't remember a thing the next morning. Yet I wanted to believe it could happen, maybe even to me!

I tried it several times when I spent the night at Grandma's, but somehow didn't seem to catch the full moon or maybe I turned my face during the night not allowing for the full effect. Needless to say, my chores were never magically completed, and I never had the mysterious experience of being moonstruck, but I thoroughly enjoyed the prospect of it all.

*Be the Duck Tip…*Believing in something always gives a person hope. Isn't that what we all need from time to time? Hope that things will get better, hope for a job, or hope for better health. Just keeping hope in your heart can keep you going. Thinking there might be light at the end of the tunnel is sometimes enough to continue. Hope is like dangling a carrot in front of a rabbit. In other words, you focus on the prize, the opportunity, the belief that things can change. Even believing in old wives' tales, though it may seem silly, offers hope of something magical.

Help! There's Too Much on My Plate!

This is a statement we hear frequently, especially during the holidays. Most of us seem to overspend, overeat, and overcommit ourselves to parties, gifts, dinners, and more. Afterwards, we have charges to pay on the credit card, are worn out, depressed, and are a little wider around the middle.

But that's not all. If we find all of this stressful, we may have also raised our blood pressure, allowed our immune system to be compromised, have higher cholesterol, headaches, body aches, gastrointestinal problems, and... Shall I go on?

That's why managing stress is so important to our health. During the holidays, it's okay to enjoy ourselves, but a little planning, moderation, and stress buster techniques are key to getting through them and maintaining good health, too. Here are my top 10 holiday stress management suggestions for you:

1. Decide what holiday events are really important to you and politely say no to the rest. If you'd prefer to spend your time with family and not overextend yourself to neighborhood and work parties, that's your choice.

2. Allow yourself time each day to simply relax, breathe, meditate, read, take a hot bath, or just be still. Even 5-10 minutes a day has health benefits and breaks the stress cycle, moving your body into a relaxation response. This is also beneficial toward long-term effects of stress.

3. Schedule a massage for yourself to aid in handling stressors that might come your way.

4. Start moving! Walk, run, dance, do yoga, stretch, go to the gym, or do whatever physical activity you enjoy, but do it!

5. Get plenty of sleep. It is recommended that adults get 7-9 hours of sleep a night. Staying up late and not replacing the hours you lost will add to sleep deprivation.

6. Set a budget for what you can reasonably spend during the holidays and stick to it! You may have to get creative and do some baking, make gifts yourself, eliminate folks off your list, reduce the amount spent on each person, exchange names, or whatever it takes so you don't have charge

card debt to pay off later. This will relieve some financial stressors.

7. When cooking for parties or holiday meals, make healthier foods that you enjoy. This will give you choices over the sugary treats we usually see on the table. Use moderation in all of your eating and drinking, as adding sugar, fats, and alcohol to your diet stresses your immune system, your gastrointestinal system, and your mood.

8. Enjoy some socialization. Humans are wired to be social with each other, and being around happy, energetic and positive people helps you feel better. When you laugh, endorphins are released throughout your body making you feel great and relaxed.

9. Express gratitude often. Appreciate what you have and remember to thank those who go out of their way to make your day better, who deliver your paper, who pour your special cup of coffee, and who help you through thousands of gestures daily.

*Be the Duck Tip…*So what can you take "off your plate" that will eliminate stressors and keep you from feeling that there's too much to do? Maybe sit down with your family and/or friends and choose what's most important to you and create activities and meals around just those. When the holidays are over, you will have more money in your pocket, feel more relaxed, and physically feel better.

A New Year's Resolution

During every December, as a New Year approaches, you will probably be bombarded by advertisements to lose weight, get in shape, rev up your metabolism, and how to look new and improved. I want to offer you something a bit different – a way to work on your inner self by 'exercising your soul'.

Working on your inner self is just as important as working on your biceps. Here are a few strategies that may help build up your 'soul's muscle.'

- **Meditation, Prayer and Quiet Time**: Look for time each day to be still, quiet, and reflect on what's going on in your life. Listen for a quiet whisper showing you the path to follow.

- Having a **Heart of Gratitude** for what you have in your life helps to keep your thoughts focused on the positives and the blessings you've been given. Some days you may be thankful for a kind word, having enough food to eat, legs to walk, a family, a job, or being able to see a sunset. These things do a 'soul' good.

- **Kindness to Others** boosts your 'feel good' emotions. When I was a child, my mom used to say, "Treat others how you want to be treated," the Golden Rule. Good advice! I like to take it a step further and think that I want to treat others how I'd like my parents, my children, my siblings, and my grandchildren treated – a form of reciprocity. Kindness bonds people, builds your soul's muscle, and simply makes it a better world.

- **Kindness to Yourself** is just as important as kindness to others. Remember, no one is perfect, not even you. Quit trying to make things so. Take time each day, even five minutes, to replenish yourself, renew your energy, and do things to keep yourself healthy. Strive for greatness, not perfection.

- **Affirmations** are positive statements that build up your belief in yourself. Sometimes negative self-talk outweighs the good things we say to ourselves. One way to counter balance that is to add daily affirmations. Write them down, put them on sticky notes, and post them where you will see them several times a day. You can even memorize them. Here are some examples:

- I choose well so I can feel well. – Nathalie W. Herrman
- I get plenty of sleep every night. My body appreciates how I take care of it. – Louise Hay
- All desires for cigarettes (or alcohol or whatever it is you're addicted to) has left me, and I am free. – Louise Hay
- I am happy, healthy and loved.
- I am great at my job.
- I am wonderfully made.
- I am enough.
- Write your own….

Be the Duck Tip…So as you get ready to settle in for another year, maybe your resolution is to build your 'soul's muscle'. Exercising your soul through meditation and prayer, taking quiet time each day for yourself, having a grateful attitude, spreading kindness to others, being kind to yourself, and practicing positive affirmations will make your soul stronger and healthier!

What If?

What if you could make a difference in someone's life today? What would that look like? What skills would you use? Who would it be?

What if you mended a broken relationship today? Who would that involve? How would you do it? How would you feel?

What if you could travel anywhere you wanted? Where would you go? Why? With whom?

What if you knew this was the last week of your life? How would you spend it? Who would you see? What would you do with your money and material things? What would you do with your time and energy? What would you like people to remember about you?

By answering these questions, you've just developed your own 'Bucket List.' These are goals that are personal, meaningful and valuable to you. They involve the most important things and people in your life.

My sisters and I used to go to a lake for one weekend every summer, and part of that weekend was writing and updating our bucket lists. We held each other accountable, encouraging each other to achieve our goals. These weekends were the best, as I got to spend time with people I love. Family is one of my values, and any time I can do things with family members, I am in my happy spot.

One of the items on my bucket list was that I always wanted to go whale watching. It was something that was very spiritual for me, as nature in its truest form leaves me awestruck. So talking about it, stating I was going to do it, helped hold me answerable. In fact, two of my sisters went with me on a trip to Canada where we, indeed, went whale watching. It was fabulous!

Writing this book was on my original bucket list. I kept putting it off, always too busy. You know how it is? But last year I decided to use the same strategies as my whale watching dream. I started telling people I was publishing it this year. I started contacting people about how to publish, and I wrote every week. By doing this, I was holding myself accountable and felt like others were, too.

Why do most people put off the "what ifs..."? We each have to answer that questions for ourselves. But no one is promised a tomorrow, and that makes me reevaluate my choices every day.

Be the Duck Tip... What about you? What's on your bucket list that you really want to accomplish? What are your dreams? Take one small step this week to move yourself closer to it. Every journey starts with one step.

Broken Angel Wings

I love to imagine that angels have intervened in my life at times of need. Maybe keeping me out of harm's way, giving me comfort in times of sorrow, and dancing with me during joyous occasions. I even collect angel figurines, angel Christmas tree ornaments, and photos of angel statues from a cemetery in Puerto Rice that I took while on vacation. For some reason, these items are meaningful to me.

The strange thing about my collection of angel statues is that every one of them has fallen off a shelf or been dropped (by me) and has a broken wing. Every one of them! I glue them back together and continue to enjoy them.

This got me thinking the other day. Why do all of my angels have broken wings? I concluded that they are lot like me – broken pieces that have been glued back together. I've made mistakes, said the wrong thing, judged others, and didn't help someone when I could have. I've lost loved ones and haven't always made the best relationship decisions. But I keep going, and have to say I am happier today than I've ever been.

I'm probably not much different from you. We all have difficult times in our lives like the death of a loved one, end of a relationship, or losing a job. We don't know how we will go on, but we do. Sometimes a kind word from another, keeping busy, helping others, or just 'time' starts putting us back together. Our broken wing gets mended. Sometimes it takes a short amount of time for the glue to dry, and sometimes it takes longer. It's all a part of our humanness.

How can we prepare for these times? Well, from what I have learned so far, striving to keep our mind, body, and spirit healthy creates a quick-drying superglue called resiliency. It doesn't mean we won't feel pain. We will. But we will have some tools, strengths, and wisdom on how to keep going. This means feed your soul, your body, and your mind with healthy and positive things.

Also, having a good support system of people that love you can help you through tragedies and trying times. These are the people who walk beside you, listen when you need someone, and push you when necessary. They will probably be the people that help you glue your wing back together.

So if there is something in your life that has caused you to have a broken wing, understand that it is not permanent. Look for the glue in your life and work toward restoring your wing so you can fly and help others when theirs' break.

*Be the Duck Tip...*Never give up. Look for the glue to help you keep going.

It's Positively Possible!

Positivity produces success and good health! Catherine H. Weber, Ph.D. states it very well. "Scientific research confirms again and again…that thinking and speaking pleasant words…create changes in our brain, elevate mood, broaden our capacity to think, help us to have a clearer perspective on life, and allow us to make better decisions. We are more creative and better problem-solvers, and have healthier relationships and well-being when we think positively."

Positivity is a way of living, not an outcome. It's when you experience emotions like joy, gratitude, serenity, interest and inspiration. Who doesn't want more of those? Living positively can transform your future.

Here are a few general tips for living more positively.

- Connect your strengths with being positive. Think about a time you felt invigorated, you loved what you were doing, or it felt meaningful. What personal strength were you using at that time?

Was it creativity, leadership, integrity, diligence, curiosity, forgiveness or humor?

- Cultivate kindness and gratitude. How we feel about others and ourselves is important to our level of happiness. So however you express your kindness and gratitude, do it as much as possible, and your positivity level will rise.

- Develop good relationships. Positive relationships affect our health, the health of our loved ones, our friends, and our communication. You become something bigger than yourself, express more joy, and have a better social life.

- Demonstrate non-violent communication. This is how we communicate by words and body language, even under stressful conditions. This will manifest kindness, love and all of the positive emotions. Some say it's even our thoughts – how we don't judge or give an opinion in our minds. It's a way of building positive relationships and creating mutual understanding with others.

- Resiliency is our developed skills and abilities to overcome adversity and deal effectively with challenges. It's how we bounce back and move forward in life. You can build your resiliency muscle.

Norman Vincent Peal said, "Change your thoughts; change your world." In fact, a ratio of five positive thoughts to one negative will shift our life in favor of better health, better relationships, and a happier journey through this life.

*Be the Duck Tip...*5 positives to 1 negative will help you lead a life of positivity!

Bibliography

Brian Luke Seaward, Managing Stress, Principles and Strategies for Health and Well-Being, Sixth Edition, 2009, Printed in United States, Jones and Bartlett Publishing, LLC.

About the Author

Kathy Hoff is a certified Stress Management Trainer, Health & Wellness Coach, and national speaker whose passion is to help people learn to manager their stress. She has her BS Degree in Elementary Education from Missouri Valley College and Master's Degree in Teaching from Webster University. Kathy lives in Lee's Summit, MO, with her husband, is marketing director for Whole Life Chiropractic, managing content director for *Around the Lake* magazine, and an on-call health educator for Health Fitness. She loves reading, walking, yoga, kayaking and mainly spending time with her triplet grandsons.